DOCTOR'S TOOLS

MARY ELIZABETH SALZMANN

Consulting Editor, Diane Craig, M.A./Reading Specialist

A Division of ABDO

ABDO
Publishing Company

visit us at www.abdopublishing.com

Published by ABDO Publishing Company, a division of ABDO, P.O. Box 398166, Minneapolis, Minnesota 55439. Copyright © 2011 by Abdo Consulting Group, Inc. International copyrights reserved in all countries. No part of this book may be reproduced in any form without written permission from the publisher. Super SandCastle™ is a trademark and logo of ABDO Publishing Company.

Printed in the United States of America,
North Mankato, Minnesota
092010
012011

 PRINTED ON RECYCLED PAPER

Editor: Katherine Hengel
Content Developer: Nancy Tuminelly
Photo Credits: Shutterstock

Library of Congress Cataloging-in-Publication Data

Salzmann, Mary Elizabeth, 1968-
  Doctor's tools / Mary Elizabeth Salzmann.
    p. cm. -- (Professional tools)
  ISBN 978-1-61613-579-9
  1. Medical instruments and apparatus--Juvenile literature. 2. Children--Preparation for medical care--Juvenile literature. 3. Children--Medical examinations--Juvenile literature. I. Title.
  R856.2.S25 2011
  610.28'4--dc22
                            2010018608

Super SandCastle™ books are created by a team of professional educators, reading specialists, and content developers around five essential components—phonemic awareness, phonics, vocabulary, text comprehension, and fluency—to assist young readers as they develop reading skills and strategies and increase their general knowledge. All books are written, reviewed, and leveled for guided reading, early reading intervention, and Accelerated Reader® programs for use in shared, guided, and independent reading and writing activities to support a balanced approach to literacy instruction.

CONTENTS

GOING TO THE DOCTOR

WHAT DOES A DOCTOR DO?

A doctor's job is to keep people healthy. When people get sick, they go to the doctor. The doctor helps them feel better.

WHY DO DOCTORS NEED TOOLS?

Tools help doctors do their jobs better than they could without them. Special tools let doctors see, hear, and measure in the body.

DOCTOR'S TOOLS

Thermometer

Stethoscope

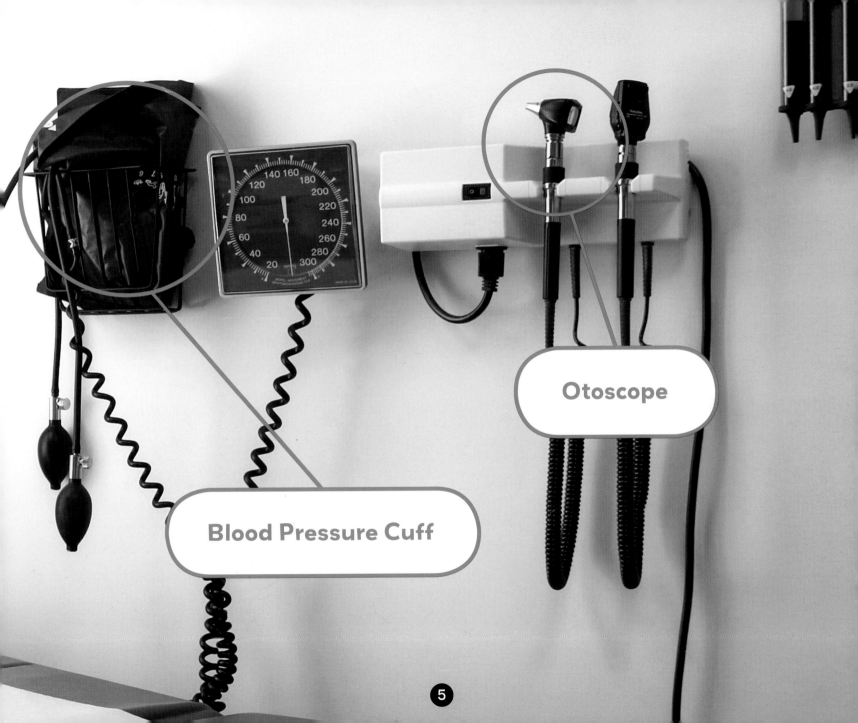

Otoscope

Blood Pressure Cuff

OTOSCOPE

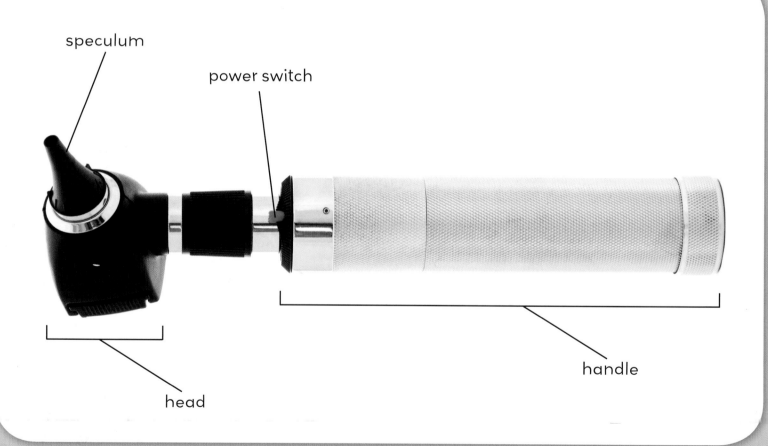

speculum

power switch

head

handle

An otoscope is used to look into the ears.

Doctors use otoscopes to check for problems with the ears. The doctor gently puts the tip of the speculum into the ear. A tiny light in the speculum shines into the ear canal.

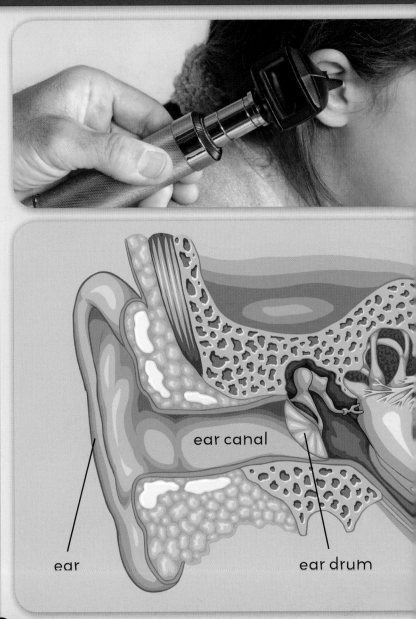

ear

ear canal

ear drum

George is having trouble hearing.
He gets his ears checked with an otoscope.

Karen has an ear infection. The doctor uses an otoscope to look inside her ear.

THERMOMETER

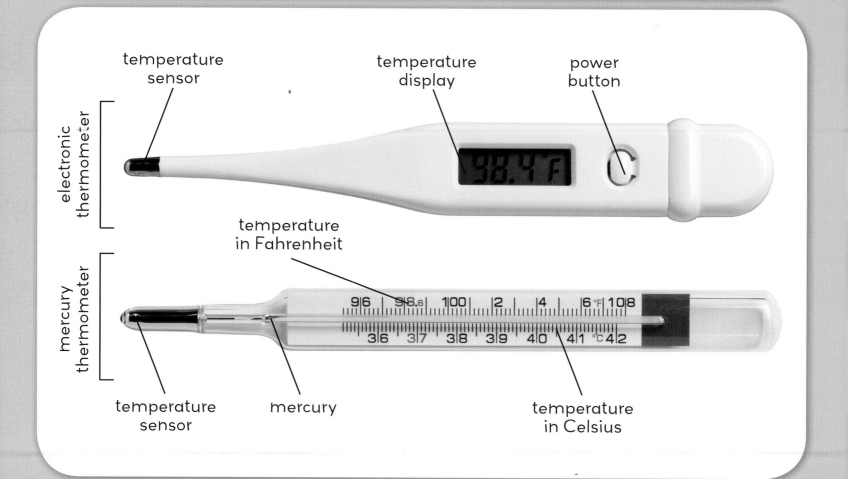

temperature sensor

temperature display

power button

electronic thermometer

98.4 F

temperature in Fahrenheit

mercury thermometer

96   98.6   100   2   4   6 °F 108
36   37   38   39   40   41 °C 42

temperature sensor

mercury

temperature in Celsius

A medical thermometer is used to measure body temperature.

The tip of the thermometer is usually placed under the tongue. The temperature sensor senses the amount of heat. Then the mercury or **electronic** display shows what the temperature is.

Alexis feels hot. The doctor checks her temperature with a thermometer.

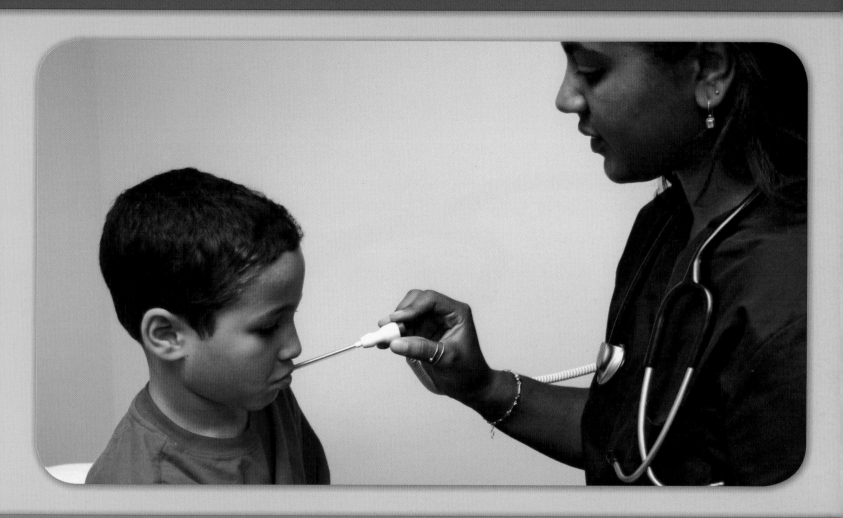

Danny isn't feeling well. He gets his temperature taken with a thermometer.

STETHOSCOPE

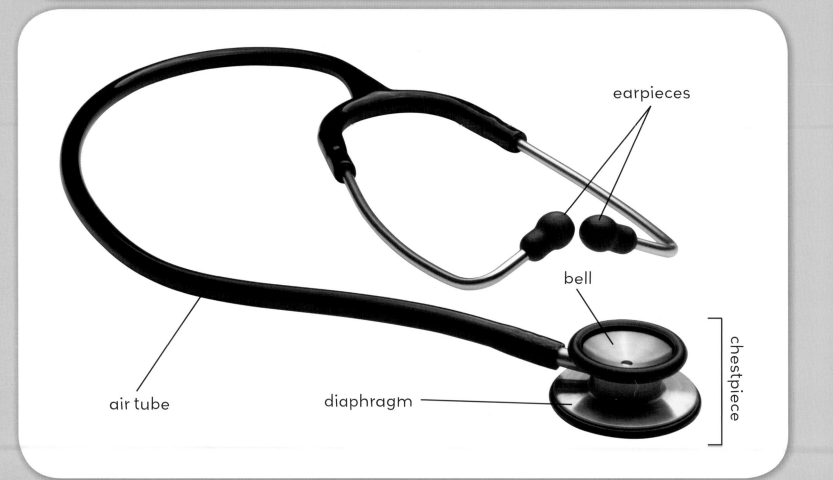

earpieces

bell

air tube

diaphragm

chestpiece

A stethoscope is used to listen to sounds inside the body.

It is usually used to listen to the heart, lungs, or stomach. The doctor places the chestpiece on the **patient's** body. Then the doctor listens through the earpieces.

The doctor lets Jimmy wear the stethoscope earpieces. He can hear his own heartbeat!

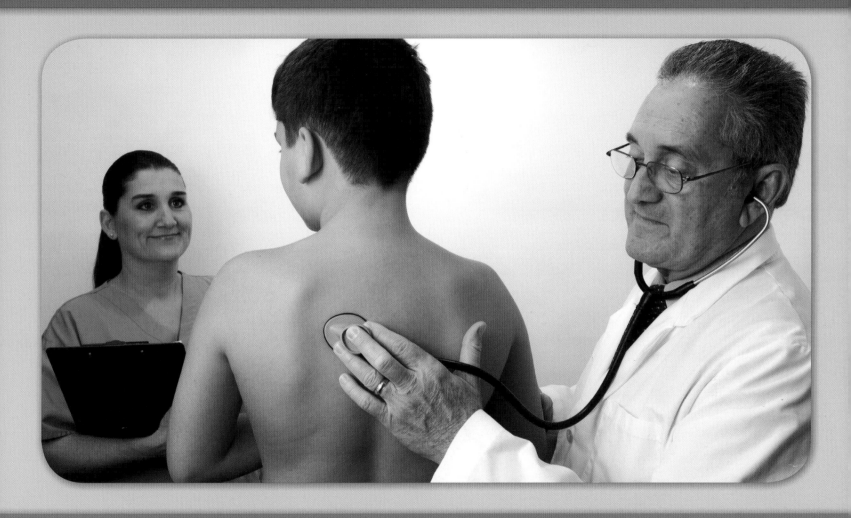

John is getting a checkup. The doctor uses a stethoscope to listen to his breathing.

BLOOD PRESSURE CUFF

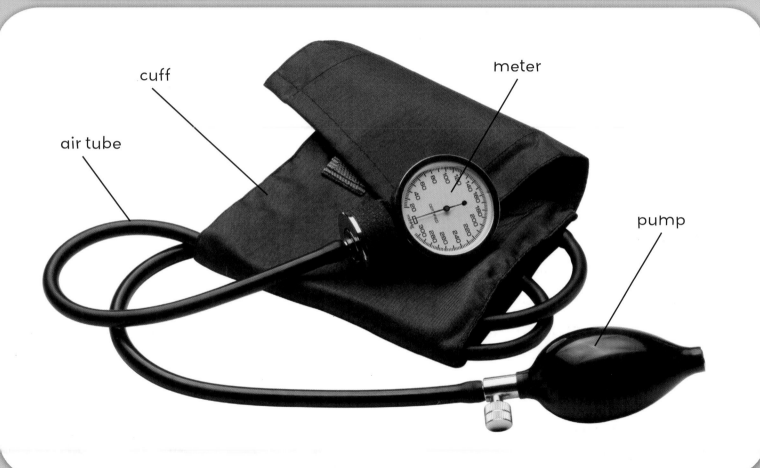

cuff

meter

air tube

pump

A blood pressure cuff is used to check the heart and the blood vessels.

The cuff is wrapped around the arm. The doctor pumps air into the cuff until it feels tight. Then the doctor slowly lets the air out. The blood pressure is shown on the meter.

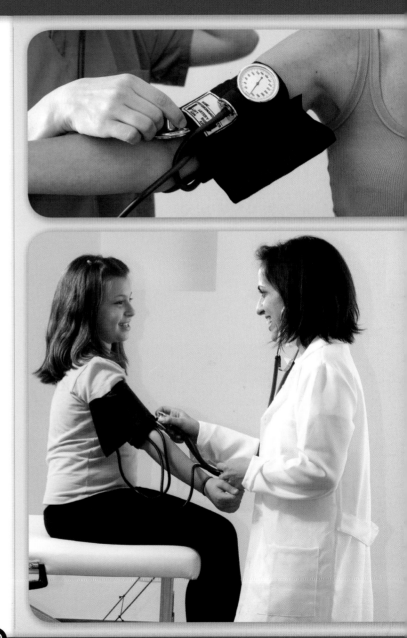

Carly just had an operation. The doctor checks her blood pressure to make sure she is okay.

Alice wants to give blood. The doctor checks her blood pressure to make sure she is healthy enough.

MATCH THE WORDS TO THE PICTURES!

The answers are on the bottom of the page.

MATCH GAME

1. stethoscope	**a.** 
2. blood pressure cuff	**b.** 
3. otoscope	**c.** 
4. thermometer	**d.** 

TEST YOUR TOOL KNOWLEDGE!

The answers are on the bottom of the page.

1.

An otoscope is used to check the ears.

TRUE OR FALSE?

2.

Thermometers can check how fast your heart is beating.

TRUE OR FALSE?

3.

Stethoscopes make it easier to hear sounds inside the body.

TRUE OR FALSE?

4.

Blood pressure cuffs are usually wrapped around the leg.

TRUE OR FALSE?

TOOL QUIZ

Answers: 1) true 2) false 3) true 4) false

GLOSSARY

blood vessel – one of the tubes that carry blood throughout the body.

electronic – powered by a very small amount of electricity that is created by electrons.

Fahrenheit – a scale used to measure temperature. It was named for Gabriel Fahrenheit.

infection – a disease caused by the presence of bacteria or other germs.

mercury – a heavy, silver-colored, liquid metal.

patient – a person who receives medical treatment.